Unique and Unusual Civil War Monuments and Memorials in the Commonwealth of Massachusetts

R. N. Chevalier

Donna Chevalier

*This book is dedicated to my co-author and wife, Donna,
who instigated this whole project.*

*It is also dedicated to Jay, our daughter,
whose actions led to the creation of this project.*

*It is also dedicated to all the men of the Commonwealth
of Massachusetts who made the ultimate sacrifice
that our nation may thrive.*

IN MEMORY OF

Therese A. Chevalier

5 JULY 1941 – 23 MAY 2022

*"When I saw the last breath leave you, I knew you were as happy
as we were sad. Through life you earned your peaceful rest."*

"You will always be loved and sorely missed."

Contents

Preface

What makes a Civil War monument unique or unusual?

For some monuments, it's their design, like the bridge and arch in Abington and the gothic design of the West Roxbury monument.

For some it's their location like being dead smack in the middle of the road in Nantucket, the bridge pillar in West Springfield and the monument of Salem, home of the infamous witch trials.

For some others it's the material used like the white bronze used in Edgartown and Salem.

And for others it's the circumstances surrounding their construction like Attleborough and Saugus.

Unlike our first Civil War monument book, *Rhode Island Civil War Monuments – A Pictorial Guide,* if we would have photographed and researched all the monuments in the Commonwealth the book would have been over 550 pages long or 5 volumes as there are more than 350. For that reason we decided to highlight a select category of monuments and memorials in this companion book.

The monuments and memorials highlighted in this book make up just under 9 percent of the total amount in the Commonwealth but reflects the imagination and diversity of ideas as well as their acceptance of the unique and different, from citizens throughout the entirety of the Commonwealth, in adulation of a common ideal, honoring the men who gave their all for the preservation of democracy.

Abington

Park anywhere along the northern end of Lake St. and you can see this monument, consisting of a bridge and square entrance arch. The bridge spans a portion of the Island Grove Pond from the end of Lake St. Two sets of stairs lead from the end of the bridge to the arch.

The concrete bridge is 299 feet long and 12.25 feet wide. The stone arch is 25 feet tall and 35 feet wide, which includes its parapet walls.

On the left side of the arch is a relief of a soldier and on the right, a relief of a sailor. On the top of the arch is the statue of an eagle, sculpted by Bela Lyon Pratt. The total cost of the project was $23,000.00.

The monument was dedicated on June 10, 1912 as part of the town's bicentennial celebrations.

The location for the monument was chosen because the grove was the meeting place of the Massachusetts Antislavery Society before the Civil War. In 1909, Moses Arnold donated a large marker to commemorate those meetings.

Moses Arnold was a successful, local business owner who was a former captain in the 12th Massachusetts Infantry when he was seriously wounded in the cornfields of Antietam. Shortly after, as commander of the local G.A.R. post, he led the effort to build the bridge and arch monument.

In 2012, during the town's tricentennial celebration, the residents voted to appropriate the funds to restore the monument. The work was done and the monument was rededicated in 2015.

A: Full view of the bridge and arch, taken from the parking area on Lake St.
B: Front view of the arch taken from the end of the bridge.
C: Rear view of the arch showing the full length of the bridge.
D: U.S. seal under inscription
E: The Soldier
F: The Sailor
G: The Eagle
H: Close-up of the eagle
I: Front inscription under the eagle.
J: Rear inscription under eagle.

ABINGTON·TO·HER·SONS
WHO·OFFERED·THEIR·LIVES
FOR·THE·VNION·1861-1865

LIBERTY·AND·VNION·NOW·AND·FOREVER
ONE·AND·INSEPARABLE

Attleborough

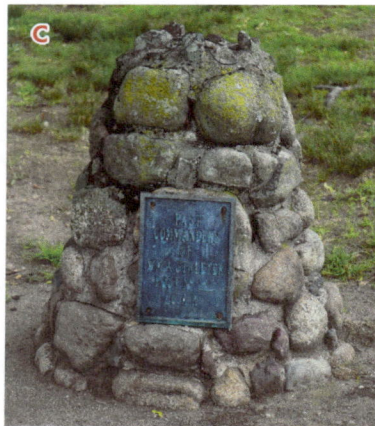

A: Full view of the monument.
B: Close-up of the flagbearer.
C: Pedestal and plaque for missing cannon.

This monument is located inside of Capron Park, accessible through an entrance several hundred yards to the right of the main entrance. It was moved to its current location in 1928, having been erected and dedicated at Monument Square (known today as Gilbert-Perry Square) on June 20, 1908.

A 7 man monument committee was appointed at the 1906 annual town meeting. At the 1907 annual meeting, the committee recommended a monument and asked the town for $7,500.00.

The town agreed as long as the committee advertised to allow as many parties to submit designs for the project.

On June 13, 1907 a Special Town Meeting was held to display all the submitted designs. At that meeting $8,000.00 was appropriated and the town authorized the committee to choose the design.

J.W. White and Sons of Quincy won the project by a unanimous decision later that year.

The monument is 35 feet tall consisting of a 10.5 foot tall granite base with a granite column and capped with a 6 foot tall Union flagbearer holding a flag. Flanking his left is a 6 foot tall sailor and to his right is a 6 foot tall soldier.

The front face of the column is adorned with an intricate relief of cross flags. Attached to the front of the monument, where the column meets the base, is an equally intricate eagle carving. On the back, opposite the flags is cross cannons and opposite the eagle, is the U.S. seal.

The granite came from the Quincy Granite Company of Quincy. The 3 bronze figures were molded by the Ames Foundry of Chicopee.

During the 1908 construction another $500.00 was appropriated to prepare the monument site. The 1908 Annual Report of the town noted that of the $8,500.00 appropriated for the monument, there was an unexpected balance of $9.95.

When the Municipal Council approved the 1928 relocation project $3,300 was appropriated by the town for the project. Demers Brothers of Attleborough was chosen to move the monument.

The monument was dedicated to the 61 men from Attleborough who lost their lives for their country.

D: Column front
E: Front of the base.
F: Back of the Column.
G: Back of the base.

H: Close-up of the sailor.
I: Full view of the sailor.
J: Close-up of the soldier.
K: Full view of the soldier.

Boston

In Boston Common, perched on Flag Staff Hill, the highest peak in the park, overlooking Frog Pond, is the monument erected in the capital city.

The base of this 75 foot tall monument is 38 feet square and consists of 4 projecting pedestals. Below the base is a subterranean foundation 16 feet deep. On the end of each pedestal is an 8 foot tall bronze figure. A female figure, representing PEACE, is holding an olive branch, looking to the south. The sailor is facing the ocean with drawn cutlass. Another female figure, representing HISTORY, is dressed in Greek garb, holding a stylus and tablet and looking upward. The infantryman is standing at ease.

On the base, between the pedestals, are bronze plaques in both high and low relief. The artist placed people, well known at the time in both the military and political theater.

The front plaque is titled "Departure of the Regiment". It depicts soldiers passing the State House steps. Amongst the troops are General Benjamin Butler and Colonel Robert Gould Shaw. Among the dignitaries are Governor John Andrew, abolitionist Wendell Phillips and poet Henry Wadsworth Longfellow.

The plaque on the right is called, "The Sanitary Commission". Visible in this plaque are James Russell Lowell and Reverend Edward Hale.

The plaque on the back of the monument is titled, "Return from the War". Celebrities seen in this plaque are General Nathaniel Banks, General

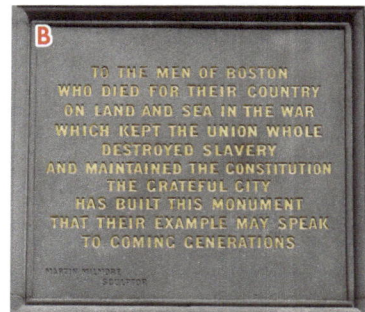

A: Full view of the monument.
B: Dedication Inscription.
C: Front bronze relief.
D: Right side bronze relief.

William Francis Bartlett and General Charles Devens, all on horseback. Among the civilians are Governor John Andrew, Senator Charles Sumner and Senator Henry Wilson.

The plaque on the left is nameless. It shows 2 scenes. The scene on the left depicts the departure of sailors and the scene on the right shows the union ironclad *U.S.S. Monitor* in a battle with a Confederate fortress and war ship.

Notice on all 4 of these bronze plaques, the incredibly intricate details of both the high and low reliefs. From the people, uniforms, weapons, flags, beards and horses (high relief) to the background buildings, walls and ships (low relief), the attention to detail, even in our modern age, is absolutely amazing.

A Roman-Doric column of white granite rises from the center of the pedestal. At the base of the column are 4 figures in high relief. They are also 8 feet tall. They represent the 4 cardinal directions, North, South, East and West. The top of the column has a square cover with carved eagles on all 4 sides. On top of that cover is a short pedestal.

Capping the monument, atop the pedestal, is an 11 foot tall bronze, female figure dressed in classic costume. She has a crown of 13 stars. In one hand she holds the flag. In her other hand is a laurel wreath and drawn sword at rest. She is AMERICA.

The monument was designed and sculpted by Martin Milmore who, along with his older brother, sculpted the monuments in Jamaica Plains and Charlestown. The white granite is from Hallowell and the bronze statues were cast in Chicopee and

E: Close-up of the lady AMERICA atop the monument.
F: Close-up of the figurine at the base of the column.
G: Close-up of the rear relief.
H: Close-up of the left side bronze relief.

Philadelphia. The president of Harvard College wrote the dedication inscription on the front.

The planning of the monument began in 1866 and the cornerstone of the monument was laid in September of 1871. It took 6 years to complete.

It was dedicated on 17 September 1877, the 15th anniversary of the battle of Antietam. A crowd of 25,000 gathered for the ceremony. Among the dignitaries in attendance were General George McClellan, General Joseph Hooker and General Charles Devens, who gave the day's key oration. The entire Massachusetts militia force paraded in Boston for the ceremony. Also in attendance to review the troops... President Ulysses S. Grant.

The monument cost $75,000.00. The grading, foundation and the expense of the dedication ceremony cost nearly the same.

I: Close-up of the top of the column with the eagles.

J: Close-up of HISTORY

K: Close-up of PEACE

L: Full view of HISTORY

M: Full view of PEACE

N: Full view of the Sailor

O: Close-up of the Sailor

P: Close-up of the shaft

Q: Full view of the Soldier

R: Close-up of the Soldier

S: Close-up of a direction figure

T: Close-up of AMERICA

Please note the incredible amount of detail in all of the figures, both bronze and granite, and the plaques and remember that it was all done by hand, without the aid of modern computer controlled machines.

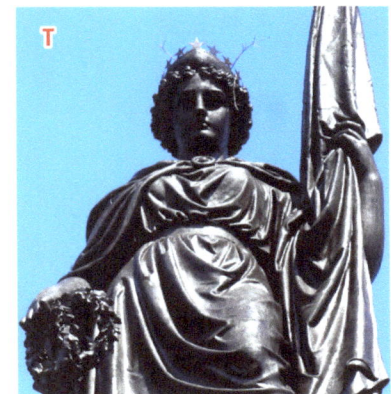

Cambridge

On 17 June 1870, this monument, designed by twin brothers Cyrus and Darius Cobb along with T.W. Silloway, was unveiled and dedicated.

This monument is 3 tiers tall and sits in Cambridge Common. Its cost exceeded $25,000.00.

The 1st tier, the base, placed upon a 3 step platform, is a square block with rectangle pedestals protruding from the 4 corners. On the 4 sides of the base, between the pedestals, are plaques.

The front plaque is the dedication plaque. The right side is a copy of The Gettysburg Address. The back is the Call For Troops and a copy of the 3 telegrams sent by Washington, DC to the government of Massachusetts. The left is a copy of General Order Number 11, which created Memorial Day.

On the 2 long sides of the pedestals are bronze plaques, 8 in all, listing those who died in defense of their country.

The 2nd tier is a roofed structure of Greek design with an arched opening on all 4 sides. Inside of the structure stands a bronze statue of Abraham Lincoln.

The 3rd tier is a carved, multi-level, square pedestal with a granite soldier standing at ease.

This monument was sponsored by 3 Grand Army of the Republic posts.

They are: William H. Smart Post 30 of Cambridgeport, Charles Beck Post 56 of Cambridge and P. Stearns Davis Post 57 of East Cambridge.

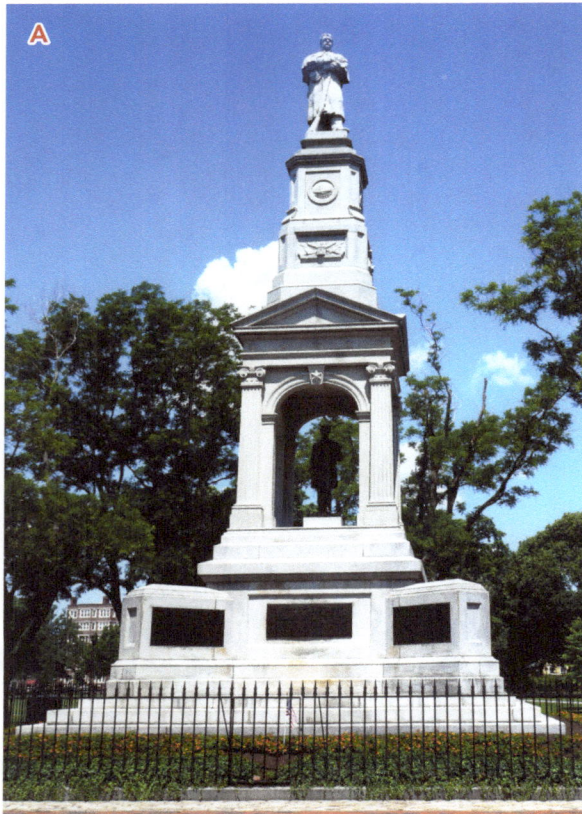

A: Full view of the monument.
B: Close-up of Abraham Lincoln.

C–F: 4 bottom emblems of the soldier's column. C: Infantry, D: Navy, E: Artillery, F: Cavalry

G: U.S. seal on the column above the Infantry emblem.

H: Eagle on the column above the Navy emblem.

I: GAR insignia on the column above the Artillery emblem.

J: Seal of Massachusetts above the Calvary emblem.

K: Full view of the soldier.

L: Close-up of the soldier.

M: Close-up of President Lincoln. (Note the details in the hands, face and suit.)

A: Dedication plaque located on the front of the base.

B: List of the dead found on the left pedestal.

C: List of the dead found on the right pedestal.

D: Plaque of the Gettysburg Address located on the right side of the base.

E: List of the dead found on the left pedestal.

F: List of the dead found on the right pedestal.

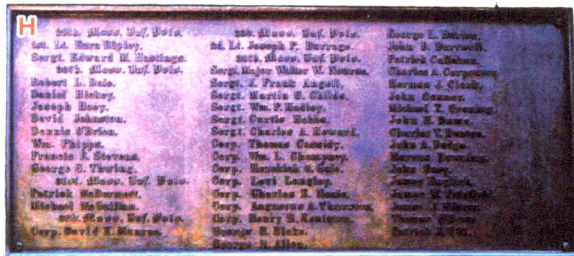

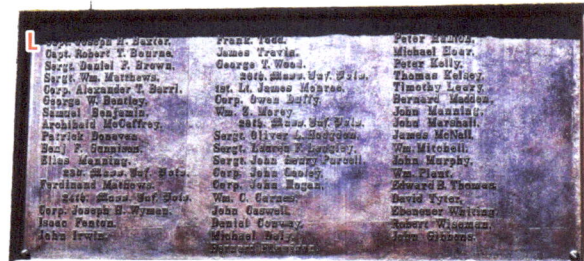

G: Call For Troops message from Washington, D.C. Below that are 3 subsequent telegrams for troops. This plaque is on the back of the base.

H: List of the dead found on the left pedestal.

I: List of the dead found on the right pedestal.

J: General Order #11, which creates the observance of Memorial Day. This plaque is on the left side of the base.

K: List of the dead found on the left pedestal.

L: List of the dead found on the right pedestal.

Charles Devens

Charles Devens was born in Charlestown, Ma. on 4 April 1820. He graduated from Boston Latin School then, in 1838, he graduated from Harvard. In 1840 he finished Harvard Law School. He practiced law in Franklin County, Ma. from 1841 to 1849.

Devens was a member of the Massachusetts Senate in 1848 as a member of the **Whig** party. He was United States Marshal for Massachusetts from 1849 to 1853. After his stint as Marshal he practiced law in Worcester until 1861.

On 16 April 1861, Devens gave a speech requesting all the young men in the large crowd to go with him to the "rescue of Washington". On 19 April 1861 he was appointed major of the 3rd Massachusetts Rifle Battalion. In July 1861 he was appointed colonel of the 15th Massachusetts Infantry and, in October, was wounded in Virginia at the Battle of Ball's Bluff.

Devens was still recovering when he was promoted to brigadier general of volunteers in April 1862 and assigned command of the 1st Brigade/1st Division. At the Battle of Seven Pines he was wounded a 2nd time.

When he returned to duty he commanded the 2nd Brigade/3rd Division/VI Corps at the Battle of

Fredericksburg. In January 1863 he was given command of the 1st Brigade/3rd Division/VI Corps.

When Major General Howard took command of the XI Corps, he appointed Devens as a division commander and Devens was wounded a 3rd time at Chancellorsville. After being wounded in this battle he remounted his horse and stayed with his men. He went to the hospital after his men had been bivouacked.

He took part in the Battle of Cold Harbor, where he distinguished himself, while commanding the 3rd Division/XVIII Corps and he commanded the 3rd Division/XXIV Corps during the final stages of the Siege of Petersburg. His troops were the first to occupy Richmond after its fall in April 1865.

From 1867 to 1873 he was a Massachusetts superior court judge and was an associate justice of the Massachusetts Supreme Judicial Court from 1873 to 1877.

From 1877 to 1881 he was Attorney General of the United States in the Cabinet of President Rutherford B. Hayes. He returned to the Massachusetts Supreme Judicial Court as an associate justice from 1881 to 1891.

Charles Devens died of heart failure in Boston in 1891 and is buried at Mount Auburn Cemetery in Cambridge.

The monument of General Devens in the photos shown here is located on the grounds of the old courthouse at the corner of Highland Ave. and Main St. in Worcester and was dedicated in 1908.

In 1917 an army training center was built on about 5000 acres near Ayer, Ma. It was named Camp Devens and, in 1931, was renamed Fort Devens. Though downsized significantly, Fort Devens is still an active military installation.

A, B: Left and right views of the full monument
C: Close-up of Gen. Devens. Notice the amount of detail of his uniform and face.
D: Note the detail in this close-up of his horse.
E–G: The 3 sides of the base.

AMERICAN UNION PRESERVED
AFRICAN SLAVERY DESTROYED
BY THE UPRISING OF A GREAT PEOPLE
BY THE BLOOD OF FALLEN HEROES

Cambridge Memorial

On a hill beyond the visitors center in Mt. Auburn Cemetery stands a memorial that seems hauntingly familiar yet strangely out of place.

The founder of Mt. Auburn Cemetery, Jacob Bigelow, designed the sphinx and, after its completion, donated it to the cemetery as a memorial to the Civil War.

Bigelow commissioned artist Martin Milmore, whose name is etched into a large variety of Civil War monuments and memorials in the region. Milmore, along with his brothers James and Joseph, carved the huge statue from a single block of granite shipped to Boston from Hallowell, Maine.

The granite block weighed nearly 40 tons and produced a memorial 15 feet long and 8 feet tall showing a combination of Egyptian and American iconology. The creation of the sphinx took place at McDonald Monument Company, located across the street from Mt. Auburn.

Bigelow said that he had chosen a female sphinx because of its "associations of repose, strength, beauty and duration," and its representation of "the ideal personification of intellect and physical force."

Bigelow continues by saying, "The same ideal form which... has looked backward on unmeasured antiquity, now looks forward to illimitable progress."

On page 16, photo A shows the full view of the memorial from approximately 50 feet while photo B shows a close-up. Photo C shows the inscription on the right side of the base.

Photos D and E at the top of page 17 show the incredible detail of the head of the sphinx. Note the eagle on the top of the Egyptian headdress.

The inscription in photo F is on the left side of

D

E

F

JACOB BIGELOW STATUIT ET DEDICAVIT

AMERICA CONSERVATA
AFRICA LIBERATA
POPULO MAGNO ASSURGENTE
HEROUM SANGUINE FUSO

G

H

I

AMERICAN UNION PRESERVED
AFRICAN SLAVERY DESTROYED
BY THE UPRISING OF A GREAT PEOPLE
BY THE BLOOD OF FALLEN HEROES

the base. It is the same inscription shown in photo C except that it is in Latin.

The flower in photo G is the Egyptian Lotus flower, which is on the front of the base and the flower in photo H is the American Water Lily, on the back of the base.

Photo I is the right profile of the memorial. Note the detail in the musculature of the lion still exquisite after facing the elements for 147 years. Also note the details in the sphinx's necklace and chest hair as well as the flowers' detailing.

Charlton

This monument stands in front of the Charlton Public Library on Main St. It was dedicated on Memorial Day, 1903.

The monument is white granite from Troy, New Hampshire and is 15 feet overall in height. It consists of a 9 foot tall obelisk placed on a pedestal which sits on a 7¾ foot square granite base. On the front of the obelisk is a high relief of a Union soldier standing at parade rest. He is looking towards the Town Common. Above the soldier is an eagle with outspread wings, clutching an olive branch. Between the eagle's wings is the shield of the U.S. Capping the obelisk, is a granite sphere lying on a blanket of leaves and flowers.

On both the left and right sides of the monument are listed the names of those men who gave their lives in the war. They are listed by regiment.

The pedestal section of the obelisk bears the dedication inscription which bears the name of the man solely responsible for the monument's existence.

William H. Dexter, a native of Charlton but a resident of Worcester, paid the $2,000.00 for the monument. It was sculpted by T.J. McAuliffe, whose work can be found all over the city of Worcester. The contractor for the project was Martin Wilson.

The dedication address was delivered by the Reverend Willard Scott of Worcester. William Dexter also spoke at the event which was attended by Civil War veterans from all the surrounding towns and from as far away as Worcester.

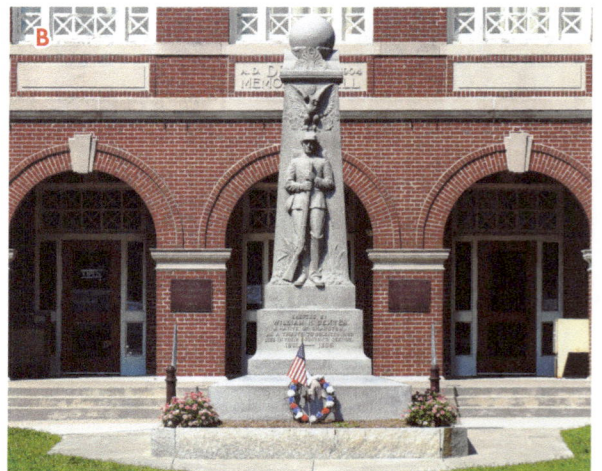

A: Close-up of relief.
B: Full view of the monument.

C: Close-up of the sphere
D: The soldier's face
E: The eagle and seal

F: Close-up of the soldier to show the detail in clothing and flesh that is still visible after 115 years

G: List of the dead
H: Back side of the monument
I: List of the dead

Edgartown

As one enters Edgartown from Main St., one can see the 32 foot tall obelisk on the right in Memorial Park (or as it's referred to on Martha's Vineyard signage… Cannonball Park).

This monument is unique in that it is 1 of only a handful of zinc statues. The monument is made up of 3 pieces held together by 1.5 inch diameter copper bolts. The white bronze (zinc) obelisk is 25 feet tall and weighs in at 6100 pounds. It was manufactured by Monumental Bronze Company of Bridgeport, Connecticut.

The obelisk's 4 sides are aligned with the 4 compass points. The north side depicts a full size image of a soldier. Below him is the national Coat of Arms. Below that is an inscription plaque. The east side has a full size depiction of a sailor with the emblem of the Grand Army of the Republic below him. There is another inscription plaque at the bottom.

The south side has a relief of the All-Seeing Eye above the flag. Below is the Massachusetts Coat of Arms then another inscription plaque. The west depiction is of a full size woman, representing the mothers, wives and army nurses. Below her is the Women's Relief Corps emblem then another plaque. This plaque contains the Masonic letters **H.T.W.S.S.T.K.S.** These letters, according to the president of the Monument Committee and Civil War veteran who was wounded at Gettysburg, Mr. E.C. Cornell, stand for **He That Was Slain Soared To Kindred Spirits**.

Below the obelisk is a granite block containing a dedication on the north side followed by the names of the soldiers on the remaining 3 sides. The final piece is the granite base. These 2 granite blocks stand 7 feet tall and weigh in at 11.5 tons.

A: Full view as one approaches the monument from Main Street.
B: North side inscription plaque.
C: West side inscription plaque.
D: South side inscription plaque.
E: East side inscription plaque.

ERECTED
THROUGH THE EFFORTS OF
ENOCH C. CORNELL
CO. H 1ST REGT. MASS. VOL. INF.

1861 HONOR ROLL 1865
CIVIL WAR VETERANS OF EDGARTOWN

FRANK ADLINGTON	THOMAS DEXTER
ELIHU BUNKER	WILLIAM EARLE
DAVID S. BEETLE	ALONZO D. FISHER
EDWARD E. BEETLE	THOMAS A. FISHER
GUSTAVUS BAYLIES	CYRUS FISHER
ENOCH CORNELL	JOHN R. FISHER
GEORGE W. CURTIS	ERIC GABRIELSON
JOHN CHADWICK	ALBION GIBBS
EDWIN COFFIN	BERIAH T. HILLMAN
THOMAS D. CLEVELAND	WILLIAM HARRINGTON
CHARLES W. CLEVELAND	EDWARD F. HEDDEN

BENJAMIN KIDDER	CHARLES NORTON
WILLIAM E. KNIGHTS	GEORGE B. ORSWELL
AARON D. LITTLEFIELD	GEORGE W. PEASE
JOHN N. LUCE	ISSAC PEASE
JOHN S. MAYHEW	PETER PEASE
CORNELIUS MARCHANT	WILLIAM C. PEASE
WILLIAM B. MARCHANT	CYRUS W. PEASE
EDMUND MORSE	JOHN N. PEASE
FRANK	WILLIAM H. PEASE
SHUBAEL	FRANCIS PEASE
ICHABOD	HENRY PEASE
DAMON V. NORT	SAMUEL PENT

THOMAS PEAKES	WILLIAM W. SMITH
JOSEPH A. RIPLEY	ELIAKIM N. SMITH
ALONZO RIPLEY	WILLIAM R. TRAVIS
RICHARD D. SHUTE	LEAVITT TRAXTER
JAMES STAPLEFORD	JAMES N. TILTON
DANIEL STARK	CHARLES M. VINCENT
WILLIAM SAUNDERS	WILLIAM T. VINCENT
IVORY SMITH	FRANCIS P. VINCENT
JAMES SMITH	CALVIN H. WILBUR
GEORGE SMITH	JOSEPH WILBUR
BENJAMIN SMITH	HENRY C. WILBUR
CHAUNCEY C. SMITH	JETHRO WORTH

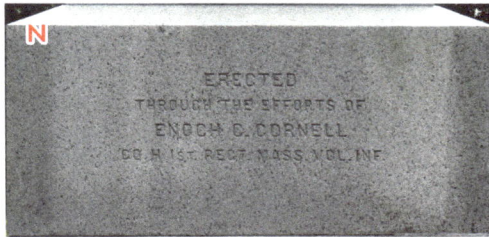

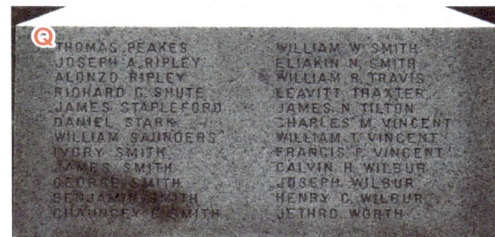

F–G: Relief of soldier and national Coat of Arms below it on the north side.

H–I: Relief of woman with the Women's Relief Corps emblem from the west side.

J–K: The south side All-Seeing Eye above the flag relief and the Massachusetts Coat of Arms.

L–M: Sailor relief and the emblem of the GAR on the east side.

N: Dedication to E.C. Cornell.

O–Q: The names of the men who went to war.

Great Barrington

This impressive monument sits in front of town hall on Main St. The monument consists of a 6 foot 8 inch woman with outspread wings, in a flowing gown, standing on a golden globe. Her right arm is outstretched and, in her hand, she is holding a crown of laurel. She is cradling an olive branch in her left arm.

The woman, known as the **Goddess Of Victory** or **Winged Victory**, is a reproduction of an ancient bronze figure discovered in the city of Pompeii. She is perched on a 14 foot obelisk style base of Portland brown stone with an inscription on the front.

Industrialist John H. Coffing was the monument committee chairman. He hired sculptor Truman Howe Bartlett and the two of them, in Europe, came across the ancient figure in Florence.

Coffing announced at a town meeting that the monument would cost no more than $5,500.00 delivered. The statue was manufactured by Thiebault & Son of Paris and completed in January 1874. Her total cost was nearly $7,000.00. Coffing paid for some of the overage himself.

She arrived from Paris in October 1874. She was placed on the lot of the Town Hall and covered with a tarp. She was left there for a year. She was brought into the new municipal building and set up in an empty room.

The monument was dedicated in August, 1876 to very little fanfare having been on display for all to see for nearly a year.

At a town meeting in 1912 a call went out to replace **Winged Victory** with a more modern figure. Word was that the citizens of the time were

A: Full view of the monument with the Town Hall.

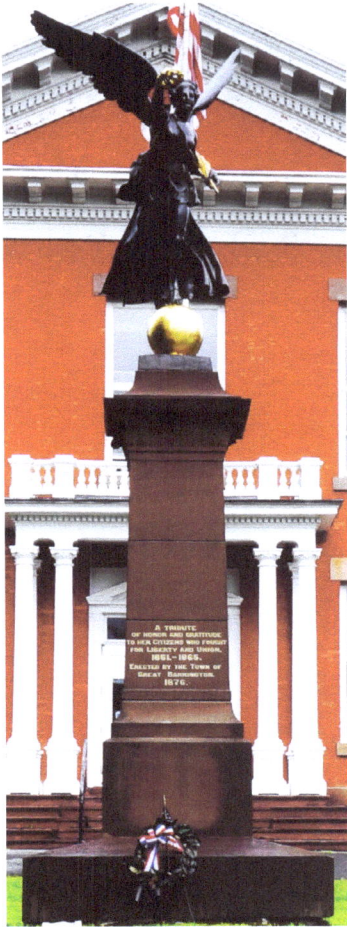

B

C

A TRIBUTE
OF HONOR AND GRATITUDE
TO HER CITIZENS WHO FOUGHT
FOR LIBERTY AND UNION.
1861.-1865.
ERECTED BY THE TOWN OF
GREAT BARRINGTON.
1876.

at arms about the lack of covering over **Victory's** breasts. This came at a time when the U.S. mint redesigned its 25 cent coin after an uproar over its depiction of Miss Liberty with an undraped bosom.

At that town meeting, Civil War veteran, and Medal of Honor recipient Frederick N. Deland asked, "What greater compliment could be paid the men who served in the Civil War from 1861-'65 than this Laurel wreath of victory?" He continued with, "Strangers coming to this town, people of broad culture and artistic tastes, who have had the opportunity to study objects of art in the old world, have paid this town many a compliment for having chosen such a subject for a soldiers' monument."

The town listened and promptly dismissed the call for change.

In 1930 repairs were made to the base. In 1953 more repairs were made to the brownstone as well as the gold leaf.

In 1997 conservation consultant Clifford Craine spearheaded another restoration project. He called the monument one of the oldest in the commonwealth.

B: Close-up of the monument.
C: Close-up of the dedication inscription.

Special note: In Photo A, the concrete benches shown in front of the monument are a memorial to a man not involved in the Rebellion in any way but they look great for photographic purposes.

24

D–G: 4 views of the **Goddess of Victory** or **Winged Victory**.

Greenfield

This monument, erected in the Common at Courthouse Square, was commissioned on 18 June 1869 and dedicated on 6 October 1870. The dedication focused on the 500 men from Greenfield who fought in the war with emphasis on the 50 men who died while in service.

A red Aberdeen granite column sits on a red Aberdeen granite base. A bronze eagle with spread wings, representing the Union, is strangling a nest of serpents, representing those in the North who opposed the war (sometimes referred to as Copperheads) and those in the South, sits atop the column.

The inscription on the front reads:

GREENFIELD
ERECTS THIS MONUMENT
IN GREATFUL HONOR TO HER
PATRIOTIC SONS
WHO OFFERED THEIR LIVES
IN SUPPRESSING THE GREAT REBELLION
AND FOR THE PRESERVATION OF THE
NATIONAL UNION
1861 – 5

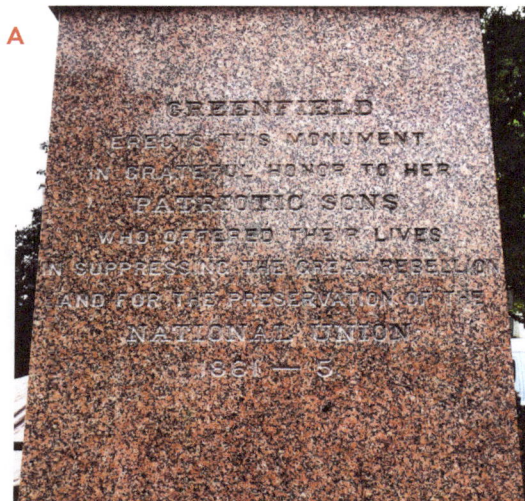

The 27 foot tall monument sits atop a 6.75 foot square concrete base.

The bronze sculpture was made in Paris. The shaft was designed and manufactured by James Goodwin Batterson of Hartford, Connecticut.

Batterson was paid $7,150.00 for the monument with another $1,752.00 spent for its installation.

A: Full view of the monument.
B: Close-up of the dedication inscription.

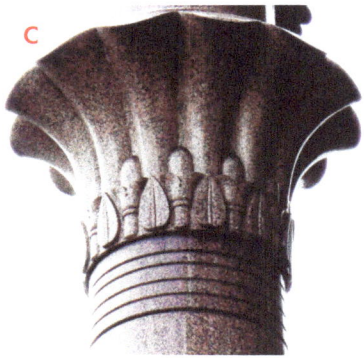
C

F

H

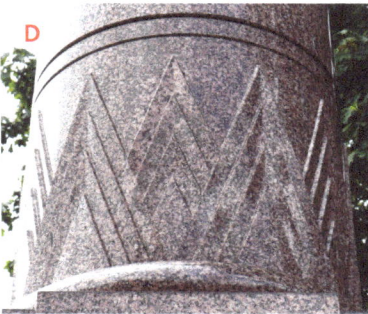
D

G

E

I

Special note of interest:

On the day Donna and I photographed this monument (4 August 2018) we learned that the city of Greenfield had allowed their homeless population to set up a community in the common where the monument is located as evident by the tents in the full view photo on the previous page. They will be there until a suitable location can be found.

C: The decorative column cap.

D: Close-up of the intricate design on the column.

E: The bottom of the column with the upper pedestal.

F: The eagle and flag.

G: The bronze eagle strangling the nest of serpents.

H: Front of the artillery gun behind the monument.

I: Side view of the artillery gun.

Marion

This memorial is located in the far left corner of Evergreen Cemetery, on Mill St. and is dedicated to the unknown soldiers of the Rebellion.

The memorial is a plot of ground 70 feet long by 30 feet on its east side by 21 feet on its west side. The size of the plot, as shown on a 1934 cemetery layout, is comparable to 7 standard size burial plots from the surrounding sections. There is a plaque on a rock on its northwest corner as well as an intricately detailed zinc cross in its center.

The cross has 4 plaques on its base, as pictured below. Photo C shows the front of the base, Photo D is the back. Photo E shows the Sons of Veterans Medal. The inscription reads: Gratia Dei Servatus, which is Latin for Preserved By The Grace Of God and the roman numerals read: 1881. Photo F is the emblem of the G.A.R.

This memorial was dedicated in 1906 and was made a reality by veterans, sons of veterans and ladies auxiliary.

After contacting the Marion Historical Commission and the Marion Cemetery Commission as well as media both new and old, no other information can be found regarding this memorial and that is one of the things that makes it one of the most unusual in the Commonwealth.

The authors speculate that the intent was to leave plots in the cemetery open in honor of those local men who are buried in unknown graves across the Civil War battlefields.

A: Full view of the cross.
B: The plaque on the rock in the northwest corner in the top picture.
C–F: Close-up of the 4 sides of the base of the cross.

Melvin Memorial

A

B

This memorial is located in the older of the 2 sections of Sleepy Hollow Cemetery in Concord.

It was erected by veteran James Melvin to honor his 3 brothers… Asa, John and Samuel. The 3 brothers were members of the 1st Mass. Heavy Artillery. All 3 were killed in the war. (see photos)

Asa is buried in Virginia and Samuel in Georgia. John and James are buried in the family plot at the other end of the cemetery.

The female figure is "Mourning Victory" holding a flag and laurel branch. She is looking down at the 3 slate tablets symbolizing the 3 brothers.

The memorial was dedicated on 16 June 1909, the 45th anniversary of Asa Melvin's death, with 88 members of the 1st Mass. Heavy Artillery present.

The memorial was rededicated on 16 June 2019, the 155th anniversary of Asa's death after a major restoration.

C

A: Full view showing the full scale of the memorial.
B: Close-up of "Mourning Victory".
C: Inscription located below "Mourning Victory".
D–F: The 3 slate tables honoring the 3 brothers.

D

E

F

Medal of Honor Recipients

Atkinson, Thomas E.

Rank and organization: Yeoman, U.S. Navy. Born: 1824, Salem, Mass. Accredited to: Massachusetts. G.O. No.: 45, 31 December 1864. Citation: On board the U.S.S. Richmond, Mobile Bay, 5 August 1864; commended for coolness and energy in supplying the rifle ammunition, which was under his sole charge, in the action in Mobile Bay on the morning of 5 August 1864. He was a petty officer on board the U.S. Frigate Congress in 1842-46; was present and assisted in capturing the whole of the Buenos Ayrean fleet by that vessel off Montevideo; joined the Richmond in September 1860; was in the action with Fort McRea, the Head of the Passes of the Mississippi, Forts Jackson and St. Philip, the Chalmettes, the rebel ironclads and gunboats below New Orleans, Vicksburg, Port Hudson, and at the surrender of New Orleans.

Casey, David P.

Rank and organization: Private, Company C, 25th Massachusetts Infantry. Place and date: At Cold Harbor, Va., 3 June 1864. Entered service at: Northbridge, Mass. Birth: Ireland. Date of issue: 14 September 1888. Citation: Two color bearers having been shot dead one after the other, the last one far in advance of his regiment and close to the enemy's line, this soldier rushed forward, and, under a galling fire, after removing the dead body of the bearer therefrom, secured the flag and returned with it to the Union lines.

All text on this page is copied directly from the official records located at **http://history.army.mil**.

Nantucket

The intersection which ends Upper Main St. is the location of the island's Civil War monument, which is the 1st monument erected on the island.

The monument was 1st proposed by Reverend Doctor Ferdinand C. Ewer at the High School Alumni supper in 1865.

In 1868, Reverend Ewer gave a lecture in the Athenaeum Hall, raising $27. This was the beginning of the monument fund.

The monument arrived on the island in several pieces on the schooner *W.O. Nettleton* on 29 August 1874 and was completed in October 1874 with the granite fence being completed during the week of 24 April 1875.

The monument was dedicated on 29 May 1875, 10 years after its conception. In total, 339 men went to war. The names on the monument, 74 in all, are the men who gave the ultimate sacrifice.

A: Full view from the end of Upper Main St.

B–E: *These 4 plaques surround the base of the monument. 1 bears an inscription while 3 bears the names of those who did not return alive.*

B: Front plaque with inscription

C: right side

D: back

E: left side

F: Front of obelisk showing the Seal of the United States below 3 rifles "at rest".

Needham

On 30 May 1902 this monument was dedicated in Needham Cemetery in the same lot where once stood a wooden monument.

The monument was erected by the Galen Orr Post 181 G.A.R. with the assistance of the Honorable Samuel L. Powers, the congressman from Newton.

The inspiration for this monument comes from a similar, yet smaller, monument in the Town of Winchester.

The overall cost of this monument was nearly $900 dollars. The money was raised by newspaper subscription.

The lot in the cemetery, which housed the original monument, was expanded from 30x30 feet to 34x43 feet.

The base of this monument is a triangular granite block 11 feet on a side. It weighs in at nearly 13 tons.

In the center of this base are 35 11-inch cannonballs. They are set in a triangular pyramid of 15 per side.

The monument, set upon the base at the corners, consists of 3 guns mounted on their breeches with their barrels slanting skyward to form a triangular pyramid. The muzzles are welded into a collar which also doubles as a support for a 4th gun which aims straight up.

Within the muzzle of the top gun is an 11-in shell with an eagle perched upon it.

The guns are 32-lb siege guns. They are 10 ft. 8 in. long with a 22 in. diameter at the breech. They fire a 7-in shell and weigh 5700 pounds each.

The guns were cast in 1849 at the Alger's Foundry then delivered to the Charlestown Navy Yard. None of these guns ever saw service.

The 4 guns and 60 shells were loaned to Post 181 by the United States government. 36 shells are used on the monument itself, 2 are set on the stairs leading to the monument and the rest used to mark the boundaries of the lot.

As recorded in the Needham Chronicle on 19 October 1901, "This loan, however, practically amounts to a gift, for in such cases the articles lent are never called for…"

On 18 April 1903 it is reported that a change was made to the monument. The round shell on which the eagle was perched was changed to a conical one which sets the eagle higher in the air and making the monument stand over 25 feet in height.

Local legend tells that even though the guns were supposed to be locked in a collar, the governing body decided they should be welded in the collar, which was done right away.

The welding rendered the guns useless for military. So, in a manner of speaking, the local government stole the cannons from the federal government.

But that's just a legend.

A: Full view of the monument.
B: Grave markers on the right side of the monument.
C: Grave markers on the left side.

D: Plaque located on the forward cannon barrel.
E: Monument from behind.

THIS
LOT PURCHASED AND
MONUMENT ERECTED
BY POST 181 G.A.R. OF
NEEDHAM DEP'T OF
MASS.
GUNS AND SHELL
DONATED BY THE
57TH CONGRESS
DEDICATED
MAY 30,
1902.

Northampton

This monument is located in Bridge Street Cemetery and is a monument dedicated to the memory of soldiers and sailors "who lie in unknown graves".

The rough cut granite slab is 10 feet tall by 4 feet wide by 1.5 feet thick. It sits on a granite base measuring 6 feet long by 3 feet wide by 1 foot tall.

The front of the monument has the dedication inscription in a flattened and polished area in the center of its face. Crossing the face of the monument, starting from the left and above the inscription, is the American flag in relief. To the right of the flag is a soldier's cap seemingly hanging from corner of the inscription area.

Coming out from the cap, again seeming to hang from the corner of the inscription area is a belt with a "US" belt buckle and, hanging from the bottom of the belt is a sheathed sword. The belt and sword hang the full length of the inscription area. On the left side of the inscription area is the relief of a rifle.

The back of the monument has a smaller inscription area. Near the top of this smooth area is the relief of an anchor and at the bottom is a stack of cannonballs and a cannon barrel. Between the two reliefs is an inscription with includes the dedication date.

This monument was dedicated on 30 May 1908 at a cost of $1,200.00.

On a personal note... I find this monument as elegant in its simplicity as it is bold in its statement.

A: Full view of the monument area. The flagpole was added in the 20th century as a memorial to all wars.
B: Close-up of the monument.

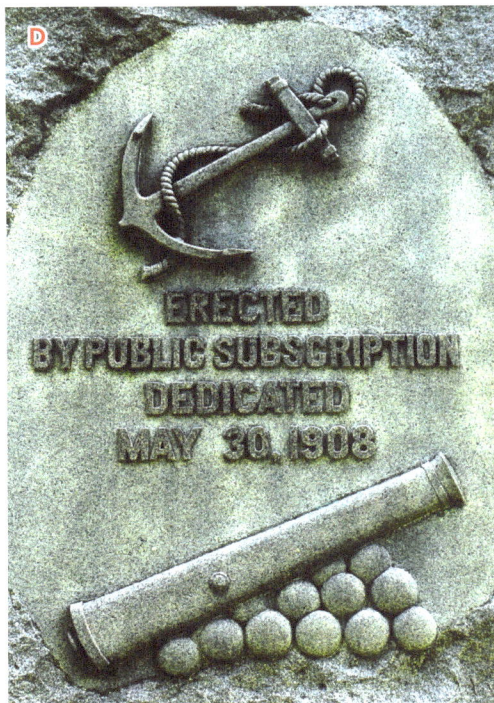

C: Full view of the back side of the monument.
D: Close-up of the reliefs and inscription on the back of the monument.

E: Close-up of the flag relief on the front of the monument.
F: Close-up of the rifle relief on the front of the monument.

G: Close-up of the sword relief on the front of the monument.
H: Close-up of the cap and belt relief on the front of the monument.

Northbridge

This monument is located in the corner of Whitinsvlle Memorial Park at the intersection of Linwood Ave. and Church St. in Whitinsville.

The monument, as a whole, was first suggested by Herman A. MacNeil, the man who would inevitably sculpt the monument with his associate, Professor A.D.F. Hamlin of Columbia University.

The pedestal of the monument, which is a triangle with concave sides and squared off corners with extended ends, sits on a 3 step, circular base. The combined height of the base and pedestal is said to be 7 feet.

The front of the monument has a depiction, carved in low relief, of a young man, looking to be a pre-teenager. He is naked with the exception of a well placed belt. His left hand is wrapped around the hilt of a sword, which is positioned as it would hang around his waist. His right hand is resting on the shield of the union.

To the upper left of the youth's head is a laurel wreath inscribed with "1861". To the upper right is another laurel wreath inscribed with "1865". Beneath the two wreaths and on both sides of the figure is the dedication inscription.

On the two remaining sides are lists of the 39 men who died in the war. The curved ends of the triangle are covered with reliefs of Greek honeysuckle, which was a common emblem of ancient funerals. The end cap shows a palm leaf. Beneath these reliefs, on the 3 sides of the 3 corners are listed the names of major battles that Northbridge men gave their lives in.

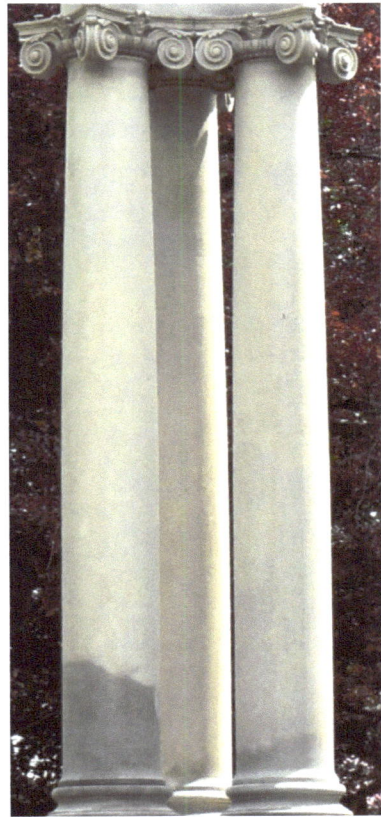

Mounted on the top of the pedestal are 3 Ionic columns topped with Roman style caps, sometimes called "Schmoozing capitals". These columns and caps stand 13 feet 1 inch tall. Resting on the columns is a triangular roof. On the roof are 3 acanthus leaves supporting a stone sphere measuring 2 feet 8 inches in diameter. This part of the monument measures 5 feet 1 inch high.

The bronze spread-winged eagle atop the stone globe is 6 feet tall and is modeled from Mr. MacNeil's pet American eagle. It's clutching an olive branch in its claws. The overall height of the monument is 31 feet 2 inches tall.

The entire monument is carved from white Connecticut granite from the Waterford quarries near New London. The work of carving the monument was performed by Booth Brothers of New York and Waterford and supervised by James Adamson and was set up by Henry Langtry, also of Booth Brothers.

The monument was dedicated on 4 August 1905 at a cost of $11,000.00 and was a gift of Whitin Machine Works and the Whitin Brothers.

Special note: In the 1st panel of names, one can see the name David Casey is highlighted. This is because even though he died years after the war, he is Northbridge's only Medal of Honor recipient.

A: Right side end cap.
B: Close-up of end cap.
C: Close-up of end cap.
D: Front of base.
E: Close-up of front relief.
F: Right side of base.
G: Close-up of names.
H: Left side of base.
I: Close-up of names.

Oak Bluffs

When you get off the Martha's Vineyard ferry in Oak Bluffs and you walk past the Steamship Authority building you will notice, in front of the park across the street, in a triangle of green bordered by park benches, one of the most unique monuments in this book. It is unique in 3 distinct ways:

1. It is one of the handful of white bronze monuments.
2. It is not only a monument but was also a functioning watering trough.
3. This monument was erected by a Confederate soldier!

When this monument was dedicated in 1891 it was located at the bottom of Circuit Ave. The sculpture is of a white bronze (zinc), 6 foot tall Union soldier. The soldier stands upon an 8 foot tall, cast iron pedestal that has 4 watering troughs attached to it, 2 for dogs and 2 for horses and pedestrians.

This monument was funded by Mr. Charles Strahan, the publisher of the Martha's Vineyard Herald. He gave a portion of each $2.00 annual subscription to the paper. He alone paid the $2,000.00 needed for the monument.

During the Civil War Mr. Strahan served as a Lieutenant with the 21st Virginia Regiment, serving under General Robert E. Lee and fighting at Gettysburg against those who he now associated with.

Even though he was ridiculed for his Confederate past, Mr. Strahan had this monument built with an aim "towards reconciliation". His vision came to fruition in 1925 when a blank plaque on the monument was replaced with a plaque paying

A: Full view of the monument.

respect to the Confederate soldiers, declaring "THE CHASM IS CLOSED".

In 1930, the monument was moved from Circuit Ave. to its present location in the triangle. The soldier fell off his pedestal several weeks after the relocation. It was brought to local plumber Benjamin Amaral, who repaired and remounted the soldier.

In 1999, a group of islanders formed the Soldiers' Memorial Fountain Restoration Inc. to repair weather damage from over 100 years of exposure to the elements.

In August 2000, the monument was removed and sent to the Conservation and Sculpture Company of Brooklyn, NY.

After nearly 5 months the repairs were complete and the statue returned to it pedestal at a cost of nearly $65,000.00.

B: Dedication plaque on the front of the fountain.
C: Plaque on the back of the fountain honoring Confederate soldiers.
D: Local GAR post plaque on the fountain's left side.
E: Right side plaque.

41

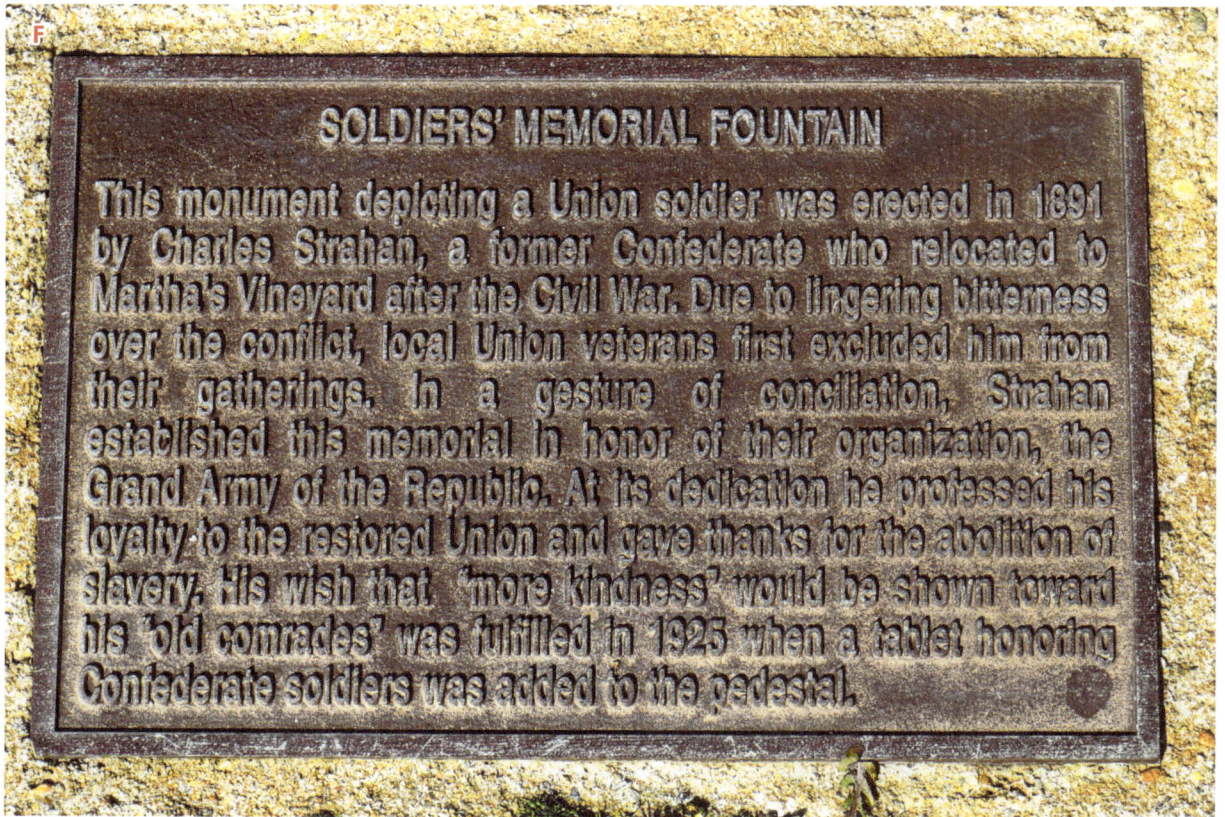

SOLDIERS' MEMORIAL FOUNTAIN

This monument depicting a Union soldier was erected in 1891 by Charles Strahan, a former Confederate who relocated to Martha's Vineyard after the Civil War. Due to lingering bitterness over the conflict, local Union veterans first excluded him from their gatherings. In a gesture of conciliation, Strahan established this memorial in honor of their organization, the Grand Army of the Republic. At its dedication he professed his loyalty to the restored Union and gave thanks for the abolition of slavery. His wish that "more kindness" would be shown toward his "old comrades" was fulfilled in 1925 when a tablet honoring Confederate soldiers was added to the pedestal.

THE RESTORATION OF THIS MEMORIAL WAS MADE POSSIBLE
BY CONTRIBUTIONS FROM THE COMMUNITY
AND THE GENEROUS SUPPORT OF
SOLDIERS MEMORIAL FOUNTAIN RESTORATION INC
SAVE OUTDOOR SCULPTURE ~ HERITAGE PRESERVATION
THOMAS & BARBARA ISRAEL
PETER NORTON FAMILY FOUNDATION
FARM NECK FOUNDATION ~ FRIENDS OF OAK BLUFFS
PERMANENT ENDOWMENT FUND FOR MARTHAS VINEYARD
RAY & THEODORA ELLIS ~ SECOND CHANCE FOUNDATION
OAK BLUFFS FIREMENS CIVIC ASSOCIATION
SLOAT HODGSON ~ SYLVIA MADER ~ STEPHEN BERNIER
OUR MARKET CORP ~ OAK BLUFFS ASSOCIATION
IN HONOR OF COL L GEORGE WILLIAMS
REGINA MCDONOUGH ~ ISLAND COMMUTER CORP
ISLAND COUNTRY CLUB ~ JUDITH & PAGE STEPHENS
DALE S COLLISON ~ EDWIN & MARY-LEE READE
DAVID MCCULLOUGH ~ MASSACHUSETTS ARTS COUNCIL
REDEDICATED AUGUST 2001

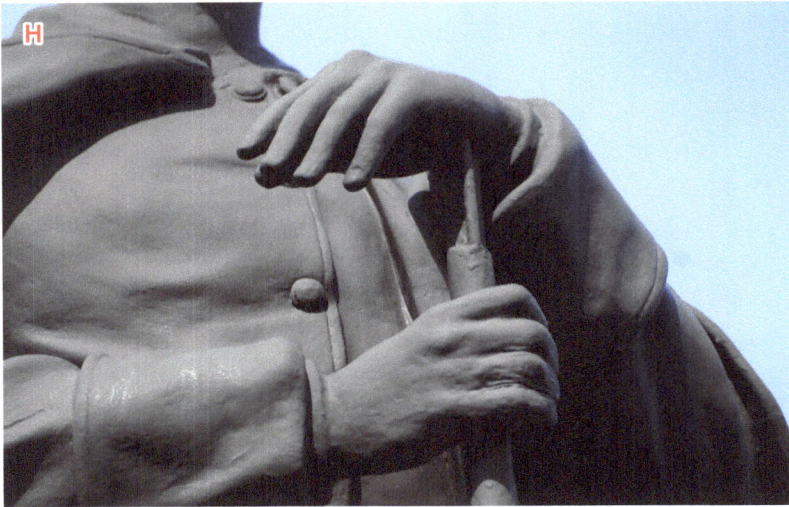

F: Plaque located in the base of the fountain.

G: Restoration plaque located in front of the monument.

H: Close-up view of the soldier atop the fountain.

I: Full view of the soldier.

J: Close-up of the watering troughs.

K: Close-up of a fountain head.

Notice, in the photos, the details in the soldier's body, uniform and fountain still visible even through the layers of rust-proof paint.

43

General Joseph Hooker

Joseph Hooker was born in Hadley, Massachusetts on 13 November 1814. He was educated at Hopkins Academy then attended West Point Military Academy, graduating in 1837.

He fought in Florida during the **Second Seminole War** (1835-1842) as well as the **Mexican-American War** (1846-1848). He received numerous accolades for bravery and, by 1848, was a Lieutenant Colonel.

After the war he served as assistant adjutant general of the Pacific Division in California. He resigned from the military in 1853 and lived in California and Oregon. He tried to rejoin the military but his request was ignored.

In August of 1861, after the outbreak of the rebellion, he was commissioned as a Brigadier General and served with General George B. McClellan's Army of the Potomac in Washington, D.C.

He 1st participated in the Civil War in 1862 during the **Peninsula Campaign**. He displayed a natural confidence in command, earning a promotion to Major General of Volunteers after serving with distinction during the **Battle of Williamsburg** and **Seven Days Battles**.

After the 2nd Battle of Bull Run, Hooker assumes a corps. command in the Army of the Potomac. He led his corps. during the **Battle of South Mountains** and at the **Battle of Antietam**, where he was wounded.

By late 1862 he took command of a grand division under General Ambrose Burnside of Rhode Island. He replaced General Burnside after the Union defeat at the **Battle of Fredericksburg**.

In June of 1863, after his defeat at the **Battle of Chancellorville**, he resigned as commander of the Army of the Potomac. He was transferred to the Western Theatre in Tennessee. There, in November, his units drove the Confederate forces off **Lookout Mountain** and helped the Union forces at **Chattanooga**.

In mid-1864 he served under General William T. Sherman during the **Atlanta Campaign**. Sherman passes Hooker over for a promotion so he requested to be relieved. In the summer of 1864 he was (relieved).

A: Photo of General Hooker during the war.
B: An entryway to the Massachusetts State House.

GENERAL HOOKER ENTRANCE

In September of 1864, President Lincoln placed him in charge of the Northern Department and he spent the rest of the war in administration in Cincinnati, Ohio.

In 1865 he was transferred to command the Department of the East and, in September, he married Olivia Groesbeck, the sister of an Ohio congressman. Their marriage ended in 1868 when Olivia died. He retired from the military that same year.

In the following years he suffered 2 strokes and was left partially paralyzed. He died in Garden City, Long Island in 1876 at the age of 64.

In the military, he had a reputation as a hard – drinking, womanizer who liked to party and had been accused of being drunk on the battlefield yet no evidence has ever been discovered to corroborate that story.

There is a legend that there was a band of prostitutes that loitered around his quarters at the encampments that were known, depending on where you hear the story, as General Hooker's Army", "Hooker's Brigade" or "Hooker's Follies". These names were shortened to, simply, "Hookers".

This is why we now call prostitutes…hookers. But it is just a legend.

C: Full view of General Hooker's equestrian statue.

D: Photo showing the intricate detail in the likenesses of both man and beast.

E: Plaque and engraving located of the front on the statue's base.

F: Plaque located on the right side wall of the stairs behind the statue in the top photo.

Peabody

A: Full view of the monument.

B: The dedication inscription.

C–E: The 3 lists of the dead. Left is the right side. Center is the back side. Right is the left side.

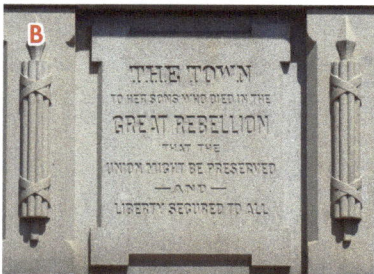

This monument is currently located in front of the town's courthouse, but that's not where it started out.

A motion was made in front of the governing body on 24 November 1879. The design and construction was given to the Hallowell Granite Company of Hallowell, Maine. This company was also contracted to construct City Hall in 1883.

Construction began on 10 November 1880 and the monument was dedicated on 10 November 1881. It was constructed in the rotary at Peabody Square.

The monument is 50 feet tall with a base that is 15 feet square. On top of the base is a square, tabernacle–type structure which, on the front, has a dedication inscription topped with an eagle. On the right side is the 1st list of those who died with the seal of the Commonwealth above it. The back has the 2nd list. On top of that was a carving of a scroll with a star above it. Carved on the scroll is the word… EMANCIPATION. The left side is the 3rd list topped with another scroll. This one says… CONSTITUTION.

On top of this is a cylindrical column decorated on the bottom and top. It is topped with a 10 foot female statue, representing "America", who's granite form weighs in at 5,300 pounds. She is a copy of Thomas Crawford's figure topping the United States capital.

"America" is standing on a

ORLANDO E. ALLEY
ROBERT ANDREWS
WILLIAM ANDREWS
SAMPSON W. BOWERS
LEVERETT C. BOYNTON
JOHN W. BOYNTON
SAMUEL BROWN 3D
JAMES H. BRYANT
PHILIP G. BUXTON
THOMAS BUXTON
JAMES BYRNE
THOMAS CAMOSEY
LEWIS P. CLARK
JOHN COSTELLO
JAMES CROWLEY
HENRY M. DeMERRITT
JOHN R. DODGE
JEREMIAH DONOVAN
JOHN FITZGIBBON
ALFRED FRIEND
FRANK GARDNER
JOHN K. GIBBS
LUKE GILMARTIN

AUSTIN A. KENRICK
ALFRED HERRICK
JOHN R. INGALLS
CHAS. P. JOHNSON
HORACE MANNING
JOHN TOPPING
JOSEPH S. MAXFIELD
GREGORY P. MORRELL
TYLER MOODY
DAVID E. LEAHY
JEREMIAH MOODY
...
NIEL MURPHY
GEORGE NASON
THEODORE NEWHALL
PAUL O'CONNELL
HENRY PACKER
OLIVER PARKER
GEORGE H. PEABODY
JAMES PERKINS
JOHN PRICE
JONATHAN PROCTOR
LEONARD REED
RICHARD S. ROOME

CHAS. H. SAWYER
PATRICK SCANNELL
MOSES SHACKLEY
ALBERT SHEPARD
WILLIAM H. SHOVE
DONALD SILLERS
WILLIAM SILLERS
BENJAMIN A. STONE
JOHN SMITH
JOHN STOTT
HORACE G. STRAW
TERRANCE THOMAS
CHARLES W. TRASK
GEORGE H. TUCKER
PETER TWISS
JOSHUA VERY
CHARLES B. WARNER
CALEB A. WEBSTER
FREDERICK WEEDEN
WILLIAM J. WHITE
GEORGE C. WHITNEY
SAMUEL WILEY
CHARLES M. WOODBURY

globe. Around the globe is a raised inscription which reads – **E PLURIBUS UNUM**, Which is Latin for **Out Of Many, One**... as in, from many colonies comes one nation

It was dedicated to the 71 residents of South Danvers (the town's name was changed to Peabody in 1868) who died in the rebellion.

The monument cost $8,000. There are also several marble tablets at the entrance to city hall honoring the men who died. The cost...$883.75.

It was moved to its present location in 1989 when the rotary was replaced by a four-way intersection. When it was moved it was disassembled into 39 pieces.

It was at this time that workers discovered that Lady "America" was never mounted to the column and she was held in place by her weight alone.

While the monument was being reassembled, a time capsule was placed inside the base. The distance of the move in 1989 was 30 feet.

F: Full view of "America" atop her globe and elaborately adorned column top.
G: The seal on the right side.
H: The eagle above the dedication inscription.
I: The scroll on the left side.
J: The scroll on the back of the monument.

Reading

A: Full view of the monument on Round Hill.
B: Close-up of the eagle atop the monument.
C: Close-up of the dedication plaque.

This monument is on Round Hill in Laurel Hill Cemetery.

It was dedicated on 5 October 1865 and is said to be the 1st monument in the commonwealth and the 3rd in the nation.

This marble obelisk is 25 feet tall and topped with the figure of an eagle. The names of the dead are inscribed on the monument, as well as the companies of the dead men along with their regiments and date, place and age of death.

Of the 411 men in 3 companies, companies A, D and G, from Reading who went war, 15 died in combat and 34 died from illness and injuries.

Members of the Richardson Light Guard fought in the 1st Battle of Bull Run. A second company of men were members of the Army of the Potomac. A third company was part of General Bank's expedition in Louisiana.

Thomas Hetler was the first man from Reading to die in the war. He was killed on 21 July 1865 at the 1st Battle of Bull Run.

Names on the front:

John H. Weston
Henry W. Wardwell
Corp. Robt. H. Weston
Geo. B. Winn
Adam Hetler
Corp. Otis S. Sanborn
Serg. Harrison Tibbetts
Mathias Gambell
Henry W. Kummer
Patrick Delay
Sydney Copeland
Daniel Berry
Thomas Hetler

Names on the right:

Samuel Prentiss
Josiah H. Smith
Chas. W. Jones
Albert Damon
Jonathon Cook Jr.
Solon D. Smith
Chas. H. Houseman
Henrie K. Parker
Robert E. Nichols
Corp. Chas. A. Dinsmoor

D–E: The front
F–G: The left side
H–I: The back
J–K: The right side

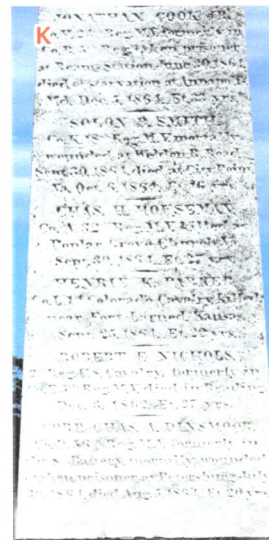

Names on the back:
Corp. Sumner B. Young
Geo. W. Nelson
John E. Robinson
Thomas E. Bancroft
Albert B. Emerson
Edward E. Pratt
Chas. L. Crouch
Chas. O. Young
S. Nelson Weston
Edward E. Nichols
Jeremiah Delay
Capt. Chas. H. Stevens

Names on the left:
Thos. S. Wakefield
Oliver S. Hartsborn
Charles Holt
Serg. Geo. J. Bartlett
Leonard Peterson
Corp. Jules R. Allen
David O'Keefe
Corp. Asa P. Tibbetts
Corp. Tobias Pinkham
Henry Damon
Serg. Asa C. Buck
John A. Barns
Benj. G. Sanborn
Moses P. Eaton

Revere

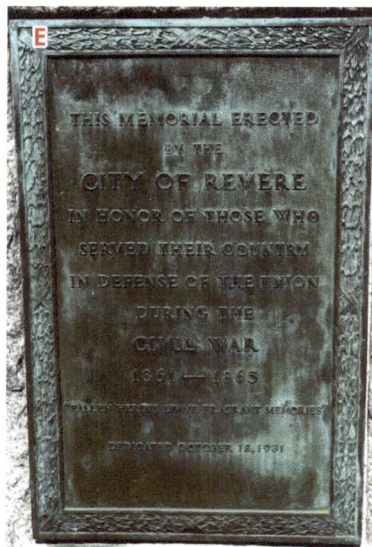

This monument, located at 249 Broadway, was dedicated on 12 October 1931.

The monument was part of the design for the American Legion Hall, which was constructed in 1930.

T.F. McGann and sons cast the soldier and plaques. The sculptor was Raymond Averill Porter, who sculpted other statues around the Boston area.

It is said that this monument is the last "standing soldier" monument to be erected in the commonwealth.

60 men from Revere, then known as North Chelsea (the name was changed in 1871), served in the war. 20 of these men having served in the Navy.

A: Close-up of monument
B: Close-up of the soldier
C: GAR emblem on the front of the pedestal
D: Close-up of "standing soldier"
E: Dedication plaque located on the back side of the pedestal
F: Plaque located on the back side of the base

Massachusetts Memorials

Public Library – 13 Main St., Hopkinton

Memorial Tower – 43 Main St., Easthampton

Salem

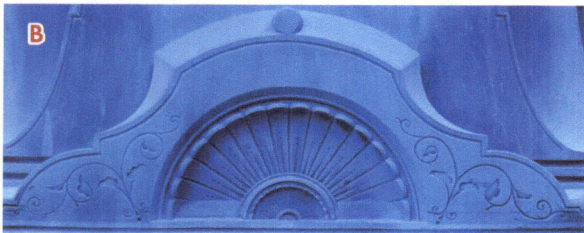

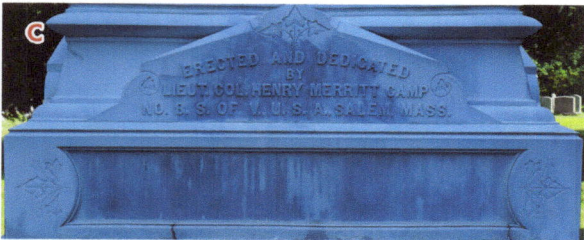

On 5 November 1886 at 1pm a 500 man parade started at Salem Common and made its way to Greenlawn Cemetery. At the end of the parade route was the Soldiers and Sailors Monument, ready for its dedication. This monument is the 1st one in the Commonwealth erected by the **Sons of Veterans** organization.

This monument is the largest in the cemetery and is one of only three that are made of white bronze (zinc).

The soldier atop the monument was manufactured by Monumental Bronze Company of Bridgeport, Connecticut, who, along with their affiliates, exclusively produced these soldiers.

Its total cost was $3,000.

In a speech by Sons of Veterans commander, D.P. Purbeck, he said,

"On those who participated, the lessons contained need not be urged, but upon the generation which has grown up since, they should be impressed. We were wrong in the very beginning. In 1776 good men established a government. God meant that it should be of all the people, by all the people, and for all the people, and we did not do it. We made a beginning, and a good beginning, but it was not a perfect work. For at the end of 80 years, we found ourselves with twice as many in bondage as we had numbered when we broke the British yoke, and we needed Gettysburg to complete the work of Bunker Hill. Bunker Hill was the promise; Gettysburg was the fulfillment."

A: Full view of the monument.
B: Front of the lower part of the obelisk.
C: Close-up of the decorative metalwork above the obelisk's lower part.
D: Detail of the intricate metalwork in the crown showing a plaque with the year of dedication.

E: Ornately decorated pedestal above the crown of the obelisk.

F–H: Right side of obelisk showing the infantry plaque (F), the Seal of the Commonwealth of Massachusetts (G) and the location of the start of the war (H).

I–K: Back view with the Navy plaque (I), an eagle, shield and arrows (J), and a short prayer (K).

L–N: Left side with the Artillery plaque (L), G.A.R. seal (M) and the location of the war's end (N).

O: Full view of the soldier. Note the lines in the fingers of the hand with the flag.

P: A close-up of the soldier showing the detail of the metalwork. Note the stitching on the cape and coat and wrinkles in the hat.

Saugus

This monument is located at 1 Main St. It is built on a keystone shaped rotary at the town's entrance.

The monument stands approximately 30 feet tall with a base approximately 20 feet square.

The granite female adorning the monument is a representation of "America". Her shield is by her side, on the ground, denoting PEACE. Her helmet is topped with an eagle, representing the Union, crushing a serpent, representing the Confederacy, in its talons. She is dressed in what appears to be Native American garb.

On the top of the base, to the left of the center column stands a bronze soldier. To the right of the column stands a bronze sailor.

The front of the base has a commemorative plaque mounted to it and the left, back and right sides of the base each have a plaque listing the names of all 163 men who fought in the war. All 4

plaques are made of bronze. Of the 163 men who served, 8 served in the navy.

The monument was designed by Melzar Hunt Mosman who also sculpted all 3 statues. The bronze statues and plaques were cast at the Chicopee Bronze Works, which was owned by Mosman who was a veteran, serving in North Carolina and Mississippi.

Before opening Chicopee Bronze Works, Mosman worked for Ames Manufacturing Company as a sculptor, producing statues for other monuments around the Commonwealth. The town of Saugus accepted his proposal over about 30 others on 18 April 1890.

The monument was a gift to the people of Saugus by Henry E. Hone of North Saugus, whose son enlisted in the 2nd Company Massachusetts Sharpshooters when he was 18. Henry left $10,000 to the town in his will for the sole purpose of this monument.

Corporal John H. Hone, Henry's son, survived the war but 15 of his Saugus comrades did not.

The monument was dedicated on 4 July 1895 to a crowd of nearly 5000 people. In fact, the monument was completed several years prior but the dedication was delayed. To this day, the reason for the delay is not known.

A: Front of the monument
B: Back side of the monument
C: Different view of the front
D: Bronze figure of the sailor
E: Seal of the United States
F: Emblem on the back of the column

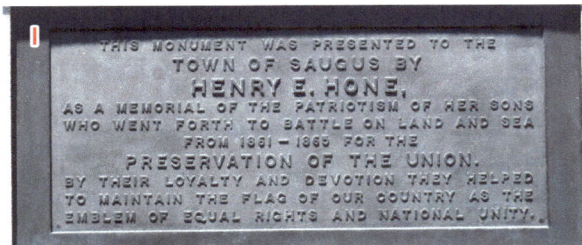

THIS MONUMENT WAS PRESENTED TO THE
TOWN OF SAUGUS BY
HENRY E. HONE,
AS A MEMORIAL OF THE PATRIOTISM OF HER SONS
WHO WENT FORTH TO BATTLE ON LAND AND SEA
FROM 1861 – 1865 FOR THE
PRESERVATION OF THE UNION.
BY THEIR LOYALTY AND DEVOTION THEY HELPED
TO MAINTAIN THE FLAG OF OUR COUNTRY AS THE
EMBLEM OF EQUAL RIGHTS AND NATIONAL UNITY.

ALBERT EATON, SAMUEL A.KNILFORD, GEORGE H.KIDDER, JACOB H.NEWHALL,
IRENA H.RHODES, ABEL HANSON, ABER HANSON, JOSEPH NEWHALL,
WILLIAM T.EATON, EDWARD ADAMSON, MARCELLUS KIDDER, HENRY R.NICHOLS,
CHARLES FAIRBANKS, LUTHER HARRIMAN, SAMUEL T.LANGLEY, WILLIAM NOBLE,
GEORGE W.FAIRBANKS, NOAH S.HARRIMAN, JOSEPH LEE, HARRISON NOURSE,
SANDA J.FISKE, ROBERT HARRISON, FREDERIC LOUIS, MILTON NOURSE,
WILLIAM L.FISKE, JAMES HERN, CHARLES H.MANSFIELD, PHINEAS KNOURSE,
WILLIAM L.FISKE, CHARLES S.HICKS, EDWIN MANSFIELD, ELLIOTT W.OLIVER,
THOMAS FLORENCE, EDWARD HITCHINGS, GEORGE A.MANSFIELD, GEORGE H.OLIVER,
PHILIP F.FLOYD, JESSE HITCHINGS, LORENZO MANSFIELD, HENRY A.OLIVER,
DANIEL FLYE, CHARLES A.HOBBS, GEORGE S.McALLISTER, WILLIAM E.OLIVER,
JOSEPH W.FLY E., WILLIAM HOLLIDAY, MOSES McALPINE, CHARLES E.OSGOOD,
OTIS A.FOSTER, BENJAMIN A.HOMAN, GEORGE H.McCLARY, A.JAMES PARKER,
WILLIAM H.FULLER, THEODORE HOUGHTON, THOMAS M.COWELL, JAMES A.PARKER,
WILLIAM E.GABRIEL, JOHN W.HOWLETT, BENJAMIN E.MARCAN, CHARLES F.PEARSON,
JOSEPH GIBBONS, SIMON HUSSEY, CHARLES A.NEWHALL, KENDALL C.PEARSON,
THOMAS GIBBONS, EDWARD A.JEFFERS, EUROPE R.R.NEWHALL, GEORGE R.PENNEY,
TRISTAM GOODALE, JAMES M.KENT, GEORGE H.NEWHALL, ALBERT PERKINS,
BINSLEY P.GUILFORD, CHARLES A.KIDDER, HIRAM A.NEWHALL, ISAAC PERKINS,
BINSLEY P.GUILFORD JR., DANIEL A.KIDDER, HIRAM H.NEWHALL, ISAAC PERKINS JR.

JOHN HENRY HONE, EDWARD CHARLTON,
WILLIAM H.AMERIGE, JAMES CHARLTON,
JOHN L.ANDREWS, WILLIAM CHENEY,
WILLIAM T.ASH, JOHN W.CHENEY,
SIMON A.ATHERTON, DAVID H.CHEEVER,
HENRY BAKER, GEORGE W.CHILDS,
WILLIAM BLANCHARD, OLIVER F.CHILDS,
ABIJAH S.BOARDMAN, BENJAMIN COATES,
ELISHA BRAGG, REUBEN R.COATES,
DAVID BRIERLY, SYLVANUS M.COATES,
AUGUSTUS W.BRUCE, JOHN H.COPP,
BENJAMIN B.BROWN JR., WARREN P.COPP,
GEORGE H.BROWN, WILLIAM S.COPP,
JOHN C.BROWN, H.CLAY CROSS,
WILLIAM W.BROWN, THEODORE CURTIS,
WILLARD W.BURBANK, WILLIAM D.CURTIS,
FRANCIS M.BUTTERFIELD, FRANCIS H.DIZER,
JOHN F.CALLEY, EDWIN H.DOWNING,
GEORGE CAMPBELL, ROBERT O.DOWNING,
JOHN F.CARLTON, WILLIAM T.DOWNING.

FRANK PETERSON, JOHN E.STOCKER,
JAMES L.PIKE, WESLEY STOCKER,
REUBEN B.PRINCE, WILLIAM L.STOCKER,
CHARLES A.RAMSDELL, WILLIAM M.STOCKER,
EDWIN W.REED, MARCUS M.SULLIVAN,
EDWARD B.RHODES, CHARLES H.SWEETSER,
WALTER E.RHODES, JOHN TIMONY,
WILLIAM W.RHODES, BENJAMIN N.TREFETHEN,
WILLIAM H.RICH, FREDERICK A.TREFETHEN,
WILLIAM C.RICHARDS, JOHN H.TWISDEN,
ALFRED B.ROOTS, THOMAS TWISDEN,
JAMES ROOTS, THOMAS TWISDEN JR.,
EDWIN ROSWELL, ELDRIDGE S.UPHAM,
ISAAC B.SCHOFIELD, FRANKLIN D.WHITMORE,
JOHN W.SEWARD, JOSEPH WIGGIN,
MOSES SPOFFORD, CHARLES H.WILLIAMS,
STEPHEN STACKPOLE, GEORGE S.WILLIAMS,
WILLIAM C.STAFFORD, ABEL R.WILSON,
EDWIN P.STOCKER, JOHN H.H.WILSON,
HARRISON F.STOCKER, SAMUEL A.WORMSTEAD.

G: America atop the monument.

H: Bronze figure of the soldier.

I: Commemorative plaque on the front of the front of the base

J: Name plaque below the sailor

K: Name plaque on the back of the base

L: Name plaque below the soldier

57

Somerville

In 1907 the town had a monument dedicated to the Somerville Light Infantry, which was later rededicated as their Civil War monument.

The years following the construction of that monument saw towns throughout the commonwealth erecting larger, more elaborate monuments.

Mayor Charles Grimmons, in his January 1907 inaugural address, made reference to the monument but expressed his desire to see a "grand, imposing monument".

On Memorial Day, 30 May 1909, this monument was dedicated. Two bronze figures stand atop a granite base approximately ten feet tall. The base bears the dedication inscription.

The bronze figures, collectively known as "American Valor", were sculpted by Henry Augustus Lukeman of New York and the casting done by the Gorham Manufacturing Company. The surrounding area was designed by architect George B. Howe. This monument on Central Hill cost $20,000.

A: Full view of entire monument.

B

C

D

E

These photos were taken in 2014. I was driving by on my way to a job and had to stop when I saw this monument.

When Donna and I went to photograph this monument for this book we found that it had been removed to make room for a new school. Further research found that the monument was undergoing restoration and rededication details would be announced. As of this writing, no information has been made available.

B: Granite base with the inscription.
C–E: 3 views of the figures showing the incredible detail involved in creating this monument.

Watertown

In an 1881 Memorial Day address, the Reverend E.P. Wilson noted that the town should erect a monument for Watertown's fallen heroes.

In June 1881, G.A.R. Post #81 formed a committee to plan such a monument and, in March, 1889, the town council announced the appropriation of $3600.

Main St. Park was chosen for the monument's location and, within five months, the monument was complete.

The monument itself was fabricated at the Hallowell Granite Company of Maine by an unnamed Italian sculptor. The soldier is a generic figure used on multiple monuments.

The cannons are 32 pounder Navy guns of 57 hundredweight. They were manufactured by the Cyrus Alger & Company of South Boston in 1849. These are the smallest "ship-mountable" cannons. Unfortunately, no information on the service history of either cannon could be found.

This monument was dedicated on 31 October 1889, Halloween, to the attendance of more than three hundred and fifty people. Business was suspended and schools were closed for the celebration.

Shortly after the monument's dedication Main St. Park was renamed Saltonstall Park.

Upgrades to the park and monument were made in 1894, 1895 and 1897.

In 1908 a bandstand was added for open air concerts.

In 1920 the bandstand was removed and a water fountain installed.

A: Full view of The Saltonstall Plaza.
B: Close-up of the statue.
C: Close-up of the soldier.
D: Dedication at the bottom of the statue.

In 1930, money was allocated for vandalism repair.

When the new town hall was built in the 1930's the monument was moved to its current location. The area it currently resides in is known as Saltonstall Plaza.

In 1981, the park, including the plaza, was renovated and, in June of that year, was rededicated.

The rededication plaque, shown below, is located in front of the cannons and reads as follows:

Dedicated to the citizens of Watertown with a prayer to Almighty God that it will forever remain a memorial of our democratic system of government and our rich cultural heritage in commemoration of the selectmen town meeting form of government.

June 30, 1981

THE BOARD OF SELECTMEN
*Thomas J. McDermott
Chairman Patrick B. Ford
Richard E. Mastrangelo*

THE SALTONSTALL PARK COMMITTEE
*Mary Louise Paliotta
McDermott   Robert Chase
Maureen Oates*

E: Dedication plaque.
F: Close-up of the information stamped into the breech.
G: Close-up of a cannon.
H: Close-up of the carving on the monument front, below the soldier
I–J: Close-up of the soldier

West Roxbury

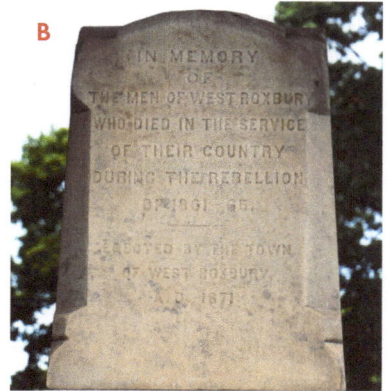

This gothic style monument is located in a triangle lot at 1 South St., Jamaica Plain (Eliot Square).

The monument was built by the citizens of the town of West Roxbury and dedicated on 14 September 1871. The construction of this monument was initiated at the annual town meeting on 28 March 1870.

The monument stands 27 feet tall with 4 arches and 4 piers. Within the arches and piers is a chamber about 4 feet square by 12 feet high. Its roof is a column and a steep dome topped with a sculpture of a soldier at rest. The top of each pier

is adorned with a multi-sided gothic cross. Each corner has a relief representing the major military components... Infantry, Calvary, Artillery and Navy. Above each arch is a name associated with the war... Lincoln, for President Abraham Lincoln; Andrew, for Governor John A. Andrew; Farragut, for Admiral David Glasgow Farragut; and Thomas, for Major General George H. Thomas.

The design for the monument was conceived by Boston architect, William W. Lummus. The soldier was created by Martin Milmore, who created the soldiers topping many monuments throughout the commonwealth as well as other sculptures in the region. The granite for this monument was procured from Clark's Island, Maine.

The cost of this monument… $15,000

Within the chamber is a stone tablet. Engraved on the front of the tablet is the dedication inscription. On the back is a list of the 23 men who died in the war. Even though the official records show that 46 men enlisted from West Roxbury, it was common practice at the time to call in men from surrounding areas to fill a town's or city's quota.

When the monument was built it was decided that only those men who actually lived in West Roxbury when they enlisted would have the honor of being forever remembered in stone.

In the event a mistake was made in the listing of the names, a blank space at the bottom of the list was left so those forgotten could be added. The blank space is still on the tablet.

The ceremony began at 4pm with a 3 division parade, followed by around 500 spectators, through town.

At 5pm the dedication began with the band playing a selection then the prayer.

George F. Woodman, chairman of the building committee, gave the opening speech. The monument was unveiled following his words.

A: Front view
B: Dedication inscription
C: Names of those who served
D: Close-up of soldier
E: Soldier at rest

E

D

F–I: The reliefs on the corners of the monument. F: Infantry, G: Artillery, H: Calvary, I: Navy
J: Cross at the top of each pier

K: Close-up of the ornate design around the column just below the dome

L: Close-up of the dome
M–P: The names above the arches

Worcester

This monument is located at Franklin and Front Streets, in the northeast corner of Worcester Commons.

The monument is 66 feet tall. Its base is 24 feet wide and, at each of its 4 corners are 4 stone cannon barrels. They are set with the muzzles buried and the breeches slightly angled towards the center of the monument.

On top of the base, at the 4 corners are bronze statues. The front, left statue is of an Infantryman. The front, right is of a sailor, representing the Navy. The rear, left statue is a Calvary soldier and the rear, right is an Artillery soldier.

The center of the monument is a large Corinthian column adorned with an elaborate cap. On top of the cap is a bronze figure. She is Athena Nike. She is wearing a flowing robe that clings to her body. Her wings are at rest as she wields a sword in her uplifted right hand and a palm frond in her left.

The monument was designed and statues sculpted by Randolph Rogers. The sculptures were cast by the Royal Foundry. Elbridge Boyden and Son was chosen as the contractor for the job.

The monument was dedicated on 15 July 1874. It was built at a cost of $50,000.00. The dedication ceremony was attended by Vice President Henry Wilson, Ex-governor A.H. Bullock, General Charles Devens, General Ambrose Burnside and the Honorable George S. Boutwell, amongst a host of others.

A: Full view of the monument.
B: Close-up of Athena Nike.

C: Calvary
D: Artillery

E: Infantry
F: Navy

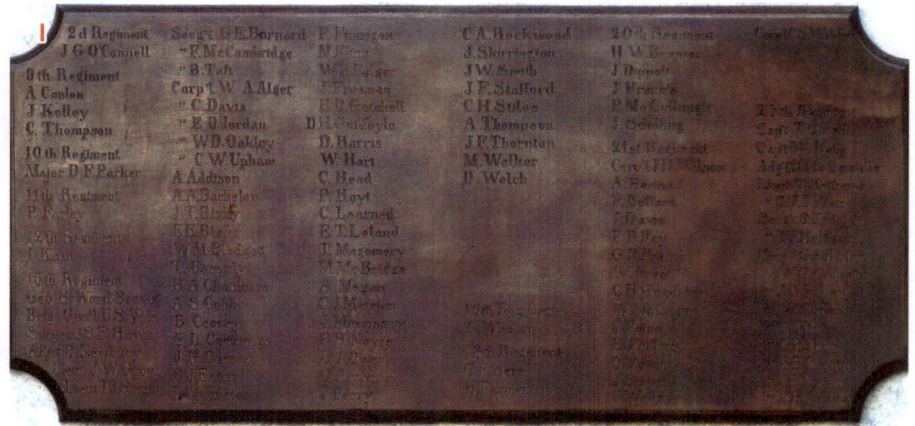

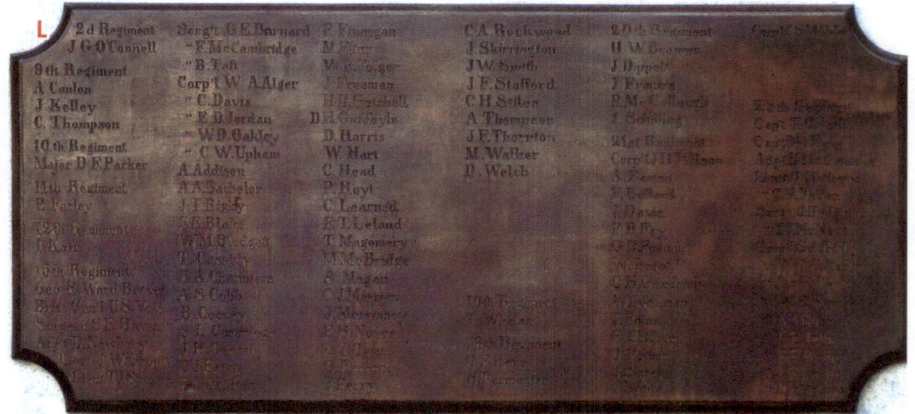

G–I: The front of the monument

    G: Top tier – Seal of the City of Worcester

    H: Center tier – Dedication plaque

    I: Bottom tier – List of the dead

J–L: The right side of the monument

    J: Top tier – Seal of the Commonwealth of Massachusetts

    K: Center tier – Governor John A. Andrew

    L: Bottom tier – List of the dead, cont.

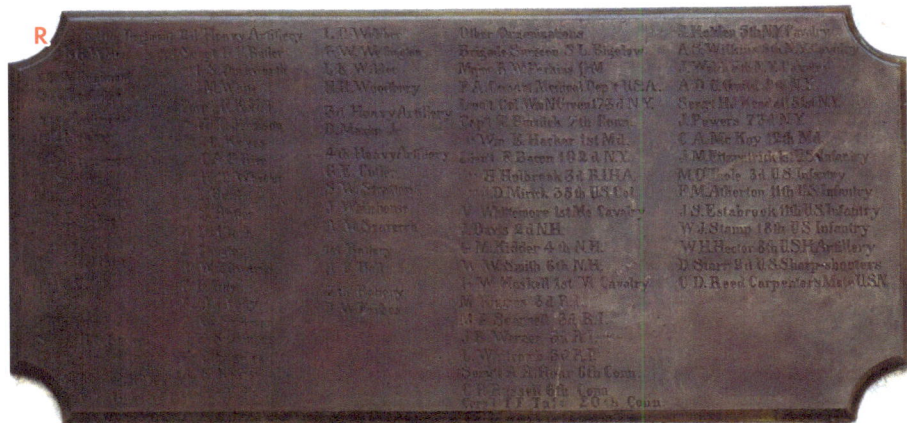

M–O: The rear of the monument
   M: Top tier – Cross rifles on a laurel wreath
   N: Center tier – Soldier helping a fallen comrade
   O: Bottom tier – List of the dead, cont.

P–R: The left side of the monument
   P: Top tier – Seal of the United States
   Q: Center tier – President Abraham Lincoln
   R: Bottom tier – List of the dead, cont.

Massachusetts Memorials

(D–F) Memorial Bridge
West Springfield

(A–C) St. Michael's Cemetery
1601 State St., Springfield

1st Unitarian Church – 90 Main St., Worcester

Memorial Hall – 30 School St., Milford

Resources

Abington City Hall
City of Attleboro – Veteran Liaison Officer
Attleboro Public Library
Boston Herald
Boston Journal
Boston Public Library
  Special thanks to Amber DeAngelis
  Special thanks to John J. Devine Jr.
Cambridge City Hall
Edgartown Public Library
Great Barrington City Hall
Greenfield City Hall
History.com
The Inquirer and Mirror newspaper
Marion Cemetery Commission
  Special thanks to Nathaniel Munafo
Marion Historical Commission
  Special thanks to Meg Steinberg
Massachusetts Civil War Monument Project
Massachusetts State House
Nantucket Atheneum
Northbridge Public Library
Northampton City Hall
Needham Chronicle
Needham History Center and Museum
  Special thanks to Gloria Polizzotti Greis
Oak Bluffs Public Library
Salem Public Library
Somerville City Hall
Somerville DPW
Watertown Public Library
Watertown Town Hall
Waymarking.com
Wikipedia.org
Worcester City Hall
Worcester Public Library